The United States Coast Guard

by Michael Green

Consultant:
Commander John McElwain
United States Coast Guard, Retired

CAPSTONE BOOKS
an imprint of Capstone Press
Mankato, Minnesota

Capstone Books are published by Capstone Press
151 Good Counsel Drive, P.O. Box 669, Mankato, Minnesota 56002
http://www.capstone-press.com

Library of Congress Cataloging-in-Publication Data
Green, Michael, 1952–
        The United States Coast Guard/by Michael Green.
        p. cm.—(Serving your country)
        Includes bibliographical references and index.
        Summary: Describes the U.S. Coast Guard, its history, missions, equipment, and
training.
        ISBN 0-7368-0472-2
        1. United States. Coast Guard—Juvenile literature. [1. United States. Coast
Guard.] I. Title. II. Series.
VG53.G74 2000
363.28'6'0973—dc21   99-053736

Editorial Credits
Matt Doeden, editor; Timothy Halldin, cover designer; Linda Clavel, production designer;
        Heidi Schoof, photo researcher

Photo Credits
Photri-Microstock, 4
Unicorn Stock Photos, 12; Unicorn Stock Photos/Dennis Thompson, 8; Brenda
        Matthiesen, 43
U.S. Coast Guard, 7, 11, 14, 16, 19, 20, 23, 24, 26, 28, 31, 32–33, 34, 37, 39, 40; U.S.
        Coast Guard/LTJG Laiman B. Miller, cover

1 2 3 4 5 6 05 04 03 02 01 00

Table of Contents

Chapter 1
The Coast Guard

The U.S. Coast Guard patrols all the ocean coasts of the United States. It also patrols the coasts of some large lakes such as the five Great Lakes. Coast Guard members use boats, ships, and aircraft to perform these duties.

Coast Guard members make sure people are safe along U.S. coasts. They perform search-and-rescue missions. They look for and rescue people whose ships, boats, or airplanes are lost at sea. Coast Guard members also enforce maritime laws. These laws apply to people operating boats or ships in U.S. waters.

The U.S. Coast Guard patrols all the ocean coasts of the United States.

The Coast Guard is the smallest of the five U.S. Armed Services. The other armed services are the Army, Navy, Air Force, and Marines. The Coast Guard works with these other armed services during wartime to keep U.S. waters safe.

Almost 35,000 men and women serve in the U.S. Coast Guard today. No other nation has a larger coast guard. The Coast Guard has about 1,400 vessels. These include boats and ships. The Coast Guard also has almost 200 aircraft. These include airplanes and helicopters.

Missions

The Coast Guard has several main duties. These duties are called missions. Search and rescue is one Coast Guard mission. The Coast Guard finds and rescues survivors of ship, boat, and airplane accidents. Survivors may be military personnel or civilians. Civilians are people who are not in the military. The Coast Guard performs more than 65,000 search-and-rescue missions each year.

Almost 35,000 men and women serve in the U.S. Coast Guard.

Another important Coast Guard mission is law enforcement. Coast Guard members enforce federal laws by patrolling coastal waters. The Coast Guard calls this maritime police work. Coast Guard members enforce many laws. They prevent people from illegally entering or leaving the country. They make sure civilian vessels meet safety standards. They also arrest people who try to bring illegal drugs into the country. The Coast Guard seizes millions of dollars worth of illegal drugs each year.

The Coast Guard also works to preserve the environment. In 1973, the Coast Guard created the National Strike Force. Members of this group clean up chemical and oil spills. These spills can harm people as well as ocean plants and animals. The National Strike Force includes three strike teams. Each team operates in a different area. The three areas are the Atlantic Ocean, the Pacific Ocean, and the Gulf of Mexico.

Coast Guard members enforce federal laws by patrolling coastal waters.

Organization

The U.S. Coast Guard includes two main groups. The largest group is the enlisted corps. About 28,000 enlisted members serve in this group. The second group is the officer corps. About 7,000 officers serve in this group.

Other Coast Guard members serve in the Reserves. Reserve members do not work for the Coast Guard full time. They often have other jobs. The Coast Guard may call Reserve members to work full time during wars or emergencies. But Reserve members return to part-time service once the war or emergency is over.

Each member of the U.S. Coast Guard has a rank. Enlisted members start with the rank of E1. The highest rank an enlisted member can reach is master chief petty officer. Enlisted members also can join the officer corps by becoming warrant officers.

Officers have higher ranks than enlisted members. This is because they have more education and training than enlisted members. Most officers start at the rank of ensign. Admiral is the highest rank an officer can earn.

Members of the National Strike Force sometimes wear special suits.

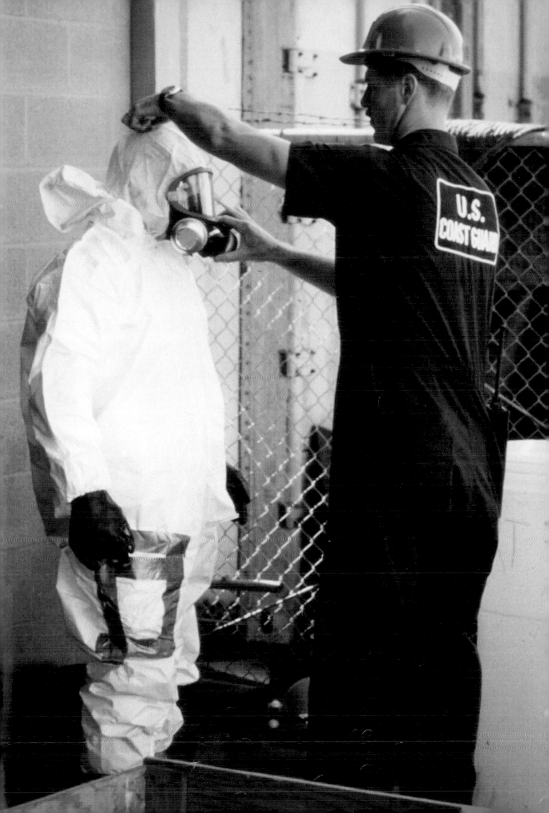

Chapter Two
History

The modern Coast Guard traces its history back to August 4, 1790. On that day, the U.S. government ordered shipbuilders to build 10 cutters. Cutter is another name for a fast ship. The government built these cutters to help collect taxes from U.S. citizens. The cutters helped the government collect taxes along U.S. coasts.

These 10 new cutters made up the Revenue Cutter Service. The U.S. Treasury Department operated these ships. But soon, government officials decided to use the cutters for other purposes. In 1794, the government started

The U.S. Coast Guard traces its history back to 1790. This date appears on the Coast Guard Seal.

The United States' first cutters belonged to the Revenue Cutter Service.

using cutters to stop illegal slave ships from entering the country. These slave ships carried African people to be sold as slaves. At that time, the United States did not allow new slaves from Africa to enter the country.

Cutters at War

In the War of 1812 (1812–1815), the U.S. government used Revenue cutters against the

British military. Crews aboard the cutters helped the Navy fight British ships on the Atlantic Ocean.

Beginning in 1822, Revenue cutters helped rid the Caribbean Sea of pirate ships. Pirates attacked civilian ships on this sea. The pirates stole the ships' supplies and often killed the people aboard the ships. Revenue cutter crews attacked and destroyed pirate bases located along Caribbean shores.

On April 12, 1861, a cannon aboard a Revenue cutter fired the first naval shot of the Civil War (1861–1865). The Civil War was fought between the Northern and Southern states. Eleven Southern states left the United States before the Civil War. These states formed a new country called the Confederate States of America.

Both the U.S. and Confederate militaries used Revenue cutters during the Civil War. The U.S. military used cutters to supply its troops. The Confederate military used cutters mainly to sink U.S. supply ships.

In 1912, a famous ship named *Titanic* struck an iceberg and sank.

Life Saving Service

In 1848, the U.S. government formed the Life Saving Service. Members of this service used vessels to rescue the passengers of wrecked or sinking ships.

The U.S. Navy operated a number of coast-watching stations at the beginning of the Civil War. It used these towers and buildings to watch for enemy ships. The Navy turned these stations over to the Life Saving Service near the end of the war. The Life Saving Service used the stations to watch for wrecked or sinking vessels. It also used the stations as bases for rescue missions.

The Life Saving Service helped almost 200,000 people from 1871 to 1914. In 1915, the U.S. government combined the Life Saving Service and the Revenue Cutter Service. The new service was named the U.S. Coast Guard.

Ice Patrol

Icebergs were a danger to large passenger ships during the early 1900s. Large ships moved so fast that they often did not have time to steer around icebergs. In 1912, a famous passenger ship named *Titanic* struck an iceberg and sank. About 1,500 people died in this accident. The U.S. government set up the International Ice Patrol that year to keep track of icebergs. The Coast Guard was in charge of this patrol.

The International Ice Patrol gave iceberg warnings to all vessels that traveled in northern waters. Not one ship has hit an iceberg and sank since the patrol began.

In 1936, the Coast Guard began an icebreaking service. The Coast Guard uses large ships called icebreakers to clear paths through icy waters. This allows other ships to pass through these waters.

Air Rescue

In 1928, the Coast Guard formed its first air rescue unit. Members of this unit used seaplanes to find and rescue survivors of ship and airplane accidents. Seaplanes are special airplanes that can land on water as well as land. Members of air rescue units entered the water after their seaplanes landed. They swam to survivors and brought them aboard the seaplanes.

The Coast Guard's air rescue units became more important as airplane travel increased. Many early airplanes crashed into the ocean. This was because these small airplanes were not as sturdy as airplanes today. Air rescue teams had to find and rescue the pilots and passengers of these airplanes.

The Coast Guard uses large ships called icebreakers to clear paths through icy waters.

World War II

The Coast Guard came under the control of the U.S. Navy during World War II (1939–1945). The Allied forces fought the Axis powers during this war. The Allied forces included the United States, the United Kingdom, Canada, and the Soviet Union. The Axis powers included Germany, Japan, and Italy.

The U.S. Coast Guard helped the Allied war effort in many ways. It provided transportation for U.S. troops. It carried troops to landing sites during invasions. Air rescue units rescued pilots whose airplanes had crashed into the ocean. Coast Guard ships patrolled waters controlled by the Allied forces.

Coast Guard work during World War II was dangerous. Enemy ships and airplanes sometimes attacked Coast Guard ships. Almost 2,000 Coast Guard personnel died during the war.

The Vietnam War

The U.S. military fought alongside the South Vietnamese military during the Vietnam War (1954–1975). They fought against the North Vietnamese military. Both sides wanted all of Vietnam to be one country. But each side wanted a different kind of government.

Vietnam has a great deal of coastline. The Coast Guard sent cutters to patrol this coastline. Coast Guard ships blocked enemy ships from bringing weapons and supplies into

The Coast Guard patrolled military harbors during World War II.

South Vietnam. The Coast Guard also sent ships to protect important South Vietnamese harbors.

In 1969, the South Vietnamese military started taking over the Coast Guard's tasks. In 1971, the last U.S. Coast Guard members left South Vietnam. But the Coast Guard left many of its cutters behind for the South Vietnamese military.

The Gulf War

On August 2, 1990, Iraq invaded Kuwait. Iraqi leaders wanted control of oil wells in Kuwait. The U.S. military sent troops to force the Iraqi military out of Kuwait. This led to the Gulf War (1991).

The Coast Guard performed several duties during the Gulf War. Coast Guard members searched supply ships entering the Persian Gulf. They made sure none of the ships carried supplies or weapons to Iraq. Coast Guard ships also patrolled the coast of Saudi Arabia. Saudi Arabia is near Iraq and Kuwait. Coast Guard ships made sure the Saudi Arabian coasts

The Coast Guard played an important role in the Gulf War.

were safe from the Iraqi military. Many of the Coast Guard members in the Gulf War were in the Reserves.

The Coast Guard also helped the war effort in other ways. In January 1991, Iraq released oil into the Persian Gulf. The Coast Guard helped other governments in the area clean up the oil. The Coast Guard also helped rebuild areas of Kuwait destroyed by Iraq during the war.

Chapter 3
Vehicles

The U.S. Coast Guard uses different vehicles to perform its missions. For cxample, the Coast Guard uses cutters to patrol coastlines and to transport people and supplies. But it also needs small boats and helicopters. These craft can reach areas large cutters cannot.

Vessels

The Coast Guard separatcs its water-going vessels into two groups. Vessels longer than 65 feet (20 meters) are called cutters. Vessels shorter than this are called boats. Cutters

Coast Guard vessels longer than 65 feet (20 meters) are called cutters.

usually are sturdier than boats. But boats can move in shallow water more easily.

The Hamilton-class cutter is one of the largest Coast Guard cutters in service. The Coast Guard has 12 of these cutters. Hamilton-class cutters are 378 feet (115 meters) long. They can reach speeds of as much as 29 knots. A knot is a measure of speed across water. One knot equals about 1.15 miles (1.85 kilometers) per hour. Hamilton-class cutters have a range of about 14,000 miles (22,500 kilometers). A range is the distance from a base that a ship or aircraft can safely travel.

The Reliance is another class of Coast Guard cutter. The Coast Guard has about 15 Reliance-class cutters in service. These cutters are 210 feet (64 meters) long. They can reach speeds of about 18 knots. Their range is about 6,100 miles (9,800 kilometers).

Patrol boats are among the smallest Coast Guard cutters. The Coast Guard has two classes

Patrol boats are among the smallest Coast Guard cutters.

The Coast Guard uses the Jayhawk for law enforcement and for search-and-rescue missions.

of patrol boats. Island-class patrol boats are 100 feet (30 meters) long. Point-class patrol boats are 83 feet (25 meters) long. Both classes of patrol boats have a range of about 2,000 miles (3,200 kilometers).

Icebreakers are the largest Coast Guard cutters. These cutters plow paths through ice in very cold waters. Icebreaker crew members make sure other ships can pass safely through icy waters. The largest icebreakers belong to the Polar class. These icebreakers are 399 feet (122 meters) long.

The Coast Guard also has about 1,400 boats in service. These include lifeboats and security boats. Boats can be as small as 16 feet (4.9 meters) long. Boats usually operate close to shore or on inland waterways.

Helicopters

The Coast Guard's most common helicopter is the HH-65A Dolphin. The Coast Guard uses the Dolphin mainly for air rescue missions. Crew members use the Dolphin's hoists to rescue people in the water. These long cables are attached to harnesses. People wear these systems of straps around their bodies. The Dolphin can travel as fast as 150 miles (241 kilometers) per hour. Its range is about 150 miles.

The Coast Guard uses the HH-60J Jayhawk for search-and-rescue and law enforcement missions. The Jayhawk can fly as fast as 262 miles (422 kilometers) per hour. Its range is about 300 miles (480 kilometers). The Jayhawk includes a powerful radar system. This machinery uses radio waves to locate objects. Radar helps Jayhawk crew members identify rescue sites and search for vessels.

Airplanes

The HC-130 Hercules is the most common Coast Guard airplane. The Coast Guard uses the Hercules for many missions. Some Hercules pilots fly surveillance missions. These pilots watch and take photographs of areas or groups of people. Some Hercules pilots fly transport missions. Pilots on these missions move military troops or supplies from place to place. The Hercules has a top speed of 375 miles (603 kilometers) per hour. Its range is about 3,400 miles (5,500 kilometers).

The HC-130 Hercules is the most common Coast Guard airplane.

The HU-25 Guardian is another common Coast Guard airplane. The Coast Guard uses the Guardian for search-and-rescue missions and surveillance missions. The Guardian has a top speed of about 520 miles (830 kilometers) per hour. Its range is about 2,000 miles (3,200 kilometers).

Surface Search Radar

Bridge

76 mm Gun

Life Boats

723

U.S. COAST GUARD

Hamilton-Class Cutter

Air Search Radar

Helicopter Flight Deck

Helicopter Hanger

Hull

Chapter 4
Training

All members of the U.S. Coast Guard receive special training. They attend classes, take tests, and perform exercises. Officers and enlisted members continue to train throughout their Coast Guard careers.

Enlisted Member Training

Enlisted Coast Guard members begin their careers as recruits. Recruits must attend basic training at Training Center in Cape May, New Jersey. There, they learn about the Coast Guard and the skills they need to be a member.

Basic training lasts eight weeks. Recruits must learn many things during this time. They

U.S. Coast Guard members must complete special training.

learn about the organization of the Coast Guard. They learn about Coast Guard rules and regulations. They also must exercise and pass physical tests.

Men and women who complete basic training become seamen. Each seaman is assigned to a one-year duty with a Coast Guard unit. There they learn about different specialties in the Coast Guard. They learn new skills. These include how to perform rescue missions and how to patrol coastlines. Seamen learn from more experienced Coast Guard members. This helps seamen decide which specialties they want to pursue.

After one year, seamen can apply to one of 23 different Coast Guard schools. They learn specialties at these schools. Some learn to become mechanics. Others learn to operate and fix computers. Each specialty school prepares students for different tasks.

Officer Candidate School

Coast Guard officers receive additional training that enlisted members do not receive. Officers must learn leadership skills. They also must

Seamen learn specialized skills while on duty.

have more formal education. Each officer must earn a bachelor's degree. Most people earn this degree in four years at a college or university.

Many Coast Guard officers receive their training through Officer Candidate School (OCS) in New London, Connecticut. Students at this school usually have already earned a college degree. Students spend 17 weeks at OCS. They learn about subjects such as natural science and law enforcement. They also learn about leadership and teamwork.

The Coast Guard Academy

Some people who want to be Coast Guard officers attend the Coast Guard Academy. This school is in New London, Connecticut. The Coast Guard Academy is a four-year program. It gives students a college education and the skills they need to become Coast Guard officers.

More than 5,000 people apply for entrance to the Coast Guard Academy each year. Some of these people are recent high school graduates. Others are enlisted Coast Guard members. Academy officials select about 250 men and women each year to attend the academy. These men and women become cadets.

Cadets spend the next four years earning a college degree and learning how to be Coast Guard officers. Their training involves class work, exercises, and hands-on experience. Cadets study subjects such as science, engineering, math, and history. During summers, cadets work aboard Coast Guard vessels. Some work aboard the *Eagle*. This

Cadets at the Coast Guard Academy learn hands-on skills aboard the *Eagle*.

sailing ship belongs to the Coast Guard
Academy. Cadets receive hands-on training
aboard the *Eagle.* They learn how to work
together to operate a ship.

About 175 cadets graduate from the Coast
Guard Academy each year. They become
ensigns. Ensigns agree to serve in the Coast
Guard for at least five years after graduation.
But many serve for longer periods of time.

Chapter 5
The Future

The need for Coast Guard services is great. Many criminals try to enter the United States by boat. The Coast Guard needs people and equipment to patrol coastal areas and arrest these criminals.

In the future, the Coast Guard will continue to play an important role in environmental protection. The Coast Guard will help to stop illegal pollution. The National Strike Force will continue to clean chemical and oil spills. This will help keep U.S. coasts and waterways clean and safe.

The United States has a great need for Coast Guard search-and-rescue teams.

Motor Life Boats

In the late 1990s, the Coast Guard began using a new kind of Motor Life Boat (MLB). In 1999, the Coast Guard had 40 of these new vessels in service. It plans to have a total of 200 by the year 2004. The Coast Guard uses these boats for search-and-rescue missions. It also uses them for law enforcement missions.

The new MLBs have features previous Coast Guard boats did not have. They are self-righting vessels. This means an MLB will turn upright on its own if it tips over in the water. The boat also is self-bailing. This means the boat removes water that washes up onto its deck. These features make the new MLBs very difficult to sink. MLBs will help Coast Guard members perform search-and-rescue missions. MLBs also will help keep Coast Guard members safe while at sea.

The Coast Guard of the future will help keep U.S. waterways clean and safe.

Words to Know

civilian (si-VIL-yuhn)—a person who is not in the military

cutter (KUHT-uhr)—a fast ship; the Coast Guard considers all ships longer than 65 feet (20 meters) to be cutters.

harness (HAR-niss)—a system of straps connected to the end of a hoist; people attach harnesses around their bodies to be lifted into the air.

hoist (HOIST)—a cable used to lift heavy objects

knot (NOT)—a measurement of speed across water; one knot equals about 1.15 miles (1.85 kilometers) per hour.

mission (MISH-uhn)—a military task

radar (RAY-dar)—machinery that uses radio waves to locate and guide objects

range (RAYNJ)—the distance that a ship or aircraft can safely travel from a base or landing point

To Learn More

Green, Michael. *Air Rescue Teams.* Serving Your Country. Mankato, Minn.: Capstone Books, 2000.

Van Orden, M. D. *U.S. Navy Ships and Coast Guard Cutters.* Annapolis, Md.: Naval Institute Press, 1990.

Useful Addresses

**United States Coast Guard Academy
Admissions**
U.S. Coast Guard Academy
31 Mohegan Avenue
New London, CT 06320-8103

United States Coast Guard Headquarters
2100 Second Street SW
Washington, DC 20593-0001

**United States Coast Guard Officer
Candidate School**
41 Mohegan Avenue
New London, CT 06320-8108

Internet Sites

United States Coast Guard
http://www.uscg.mil

United States Coast Guard Academy
http://www.cga.edu

Vessels and Aircraft Data Sheets
http://www.uscg.mil/datashcct/dataindx.htm

Welcome to the Coast Guard
http://militarycareers.com/occ/coaintro.htm

Index